A Special Gift

For

_____

From

_____

Date

_____

Fine Art by Jane Wooster Scott
provided by Superstock.

Quilts and decorative elements
courtesy of Lori Quandt Emmans

Copyright © 1997
Brownlow Publishing Company
6309 Airport Freeway
Fort Worth, Texas 76117

ISBN : 1-57051-161-6

Design : Koechel Peterson & Associates
Printed in Singapore

FROM

Friend to Friend

Brownlow

Brownlow Publishing Company, Inc.

Faithful Friends
For My Secret Pal
From Friend to Friend
Grandmothers Are for Loving
Mother—The Heart of the Home
My Sister, My Friend
Precious Are the Promises
Quiet Moments of Inspiration
Quilted Hearts ❦ Rose Petals
Soft As the Voice of an Angel
The Night the Angels Sang
'Tis Christmas Once Again

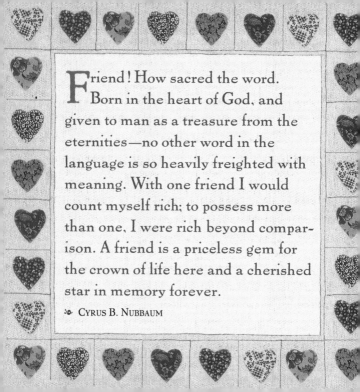

Friend! How sacred the word. Born in the heart of God, and given to man as a treasure from the eternities—no other word in the language is so heavily freighted with meaning. With one friend I would count myself rich; to possess more than one, I were rich beyond comparison. A friend is a priceless gem for the crown of life here and a cherished star in memory forever.

➤ CYRUS B. NUBBAUM

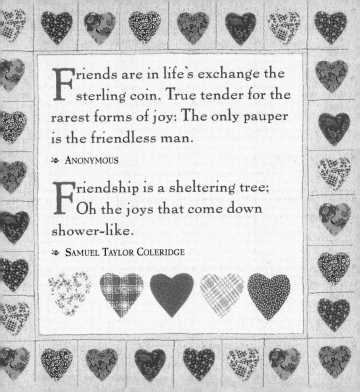

Friends are in life's exchange the sterling coin, True tender for the rarest forms of joy: The only pauper is the friendless man.

❧ ANONYMOUS

Friendship is a sheltering tree; Oh the joys that come down shower-like.

❧ SAMUEL TAYLOR COLERIDGE

A FRIEND IN NEED

"A friend in need,"
my neighbor said to me—
"A friend indeed
is what I mean to be;
In time of trouble
I will come to you
And in the hour of need
you'll find me true."

I thought a bit,
and took him by the hand;
"My friend," said I,
"you do not understand
The inner meaning
of that simple rhyme—
A friend is what the heart
needs all the time."

HENRY VAN DYKE

Each friend represents a world in us, a world possibly not born until they arrive, and it is only by this meeting that a new world is born.

ANAIS NIN

Spin carefully, spin prayerfully, but leave the thread to God.

AMERICAN PROVERB

Wounds from a friend can be trusted, but an enemy multiplies kisses.

▸ PROVERBS 27:6

Sooner or later you've heard all your best friends have to say. Then comes the tolerance of real love.

▸ NED ROREN

The shifts of fortune test the reliability of friends.

▸ CICERO

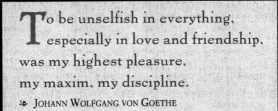

To be unselfish in everything,
especially in love and friendship,
was my highest pleasure,
my maxim, my discipline.

❧ JOHANN WOLFGANG VON GOETHE

My friend, judge not me,
Thou seest I judge not thee.

❧ WILLIAM CAMDEN

In Tune

I don't remember when I first began to call you "friend." One day, I only know, the vague companionship that I'd seen grow so imperceptibly, turned gold, and ran in tune with all I'd thought or dared to plan. Since then, you've been to me like music, low, yet clear; a fire that throws its warm, bright glow on me as on each woman, child, and man, and common thing that lies within its rays.

You've been like wholesome food that
stays the cry of hungry, groping minds;
and like a star—a self-sufficient star—
you make me raise my utmost being to
a higher sky, in tune, like you, with
earth, yet wide, and far.

FLORENCE STEIGERWALT

Friends are too valuable not to hold them close to the soul. That being where they belong, we should do more than keep a precious place reserved for them—we should grip them with our love, thoughtfulness and gratitude. They can be held. For the right kind of people are not apt to pull away from a person who demonstrates that he is on their side.

❧ Anonymous

He is a friend who, in dubious circumstances, aids in deeds when deeds are necessary.

  PLAUTUS

Friendship, like the immortality of the soul, is too good to be believed. When friendships are real, they are not glass threads or frost-work, but the solidest thing we know.

  RALPH WALDO EMERSON

A man that has friends must show himself friendly: and there is a friend that sticks closer than a brother.

PROVERBS 18:24

Friendship that flows from the heart cannot be frozen by adversity, as the water that flows from the spring cannot congeal in winter.

JAMES FENIMORE COOPER

Fate chooses our relatives, we choose our friends.

JACQUES DELILLE

Yes'm old friends
is always best,
'less you can catch a new one
that's fit to make
an old one out of.

SARAH ORNE JEWETT

A ROSE TO THE LIVING

A rose to the living is more than
Sumptuous wreaths to the dead;
In filling love's infinite store,
A rose to the living is more,
If graciously given before
The hungering spirit is fed—
A rose to the living is more than
Sumptuous wreaths to the dead.

❧ NIXON WATERMAN

For none of us lives to himself alone and none of us dies to himself alone.

ROMANS 14:7

The loftiest friendships have no commercial element in them; to the contrary, they are founded on sacrifice. They neither expect nor desire gift for gift or service for service. No bushel of friendship for a bushel of favors.

  SARAH B. COOPER

Go often to the house of thy friend, for weeds choke up the unused path.

❧ SCANDINAVIAN PROVERB

Friendship is a word, the very sight of which in print makes the heart warm.

❧ AUGUSTINE BIRRELL

Something like home that is not home is to be desired, it is found in the house of a friend.

❧ SIR W. TEMPLE

True friendship is no gourd, springing in a night and withering in a day.

❧ CHARLOTTE BRONTË

The finger of God touches your life when you make a friend.

❧ MARY DAWSON HUGHES

The need for friends is imperative. It is not good for us to be friendless. We were made to give and to receive, to help and to be helped, to encourage and to be encouraged—to feel a bond with others. Standing alone can never satisfy. Our nature requires a tie to faithful others. We call it friendship.

LEROY BROWNLOW

You must therefore
love me, myself, and not
my circumstances, if we
are to be real friends.

CICERO

Learn to greet your friends
with a smile; they carry too
many frowns in their own heart
to be bothered with yours.

MARY ALLETTE AYER

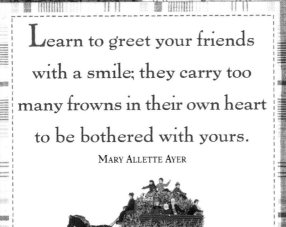

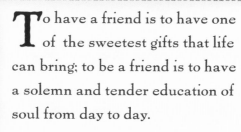

To have a friend is to have one
of the sweetest gifts that life
can bring; to be a friend is to have
a solemn and tender education of
soul from day to day.

❧ AMY ROBERTSON BROWN

Be slow in choosing a friend, slower in changing.

BENJAMIN FRANKLIN

Go home to your family and tell them how much the Lord has done for you, and how he has had mercy on you.

MARK 5:19

Animals are such agreeable friends, they ask no questions, they pass no criticisms.

GEORGE ELIOT

We cannot tell the precise moment when friendship is formed. As in filling a vessel drop by drop, there is at last a drop which makes it run over; so in a series of kindnesses there is at last one which makes the heart run over.

SAMUEL JOHNSON

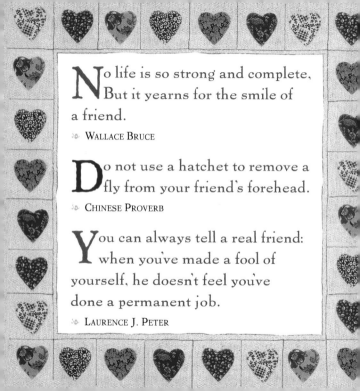

No life is so strong and complete,
But it yearns for the smile of
a friend.

WALLACE BRUCE

Do not use a hatchet to remove a
fly from your friend's forehead.

CHINESE PROVERB

You can always tell a real friend:
when you've made a fool of
yourself, he doesn't feel you've
done a permanent job.

LAURENCE J. PETER

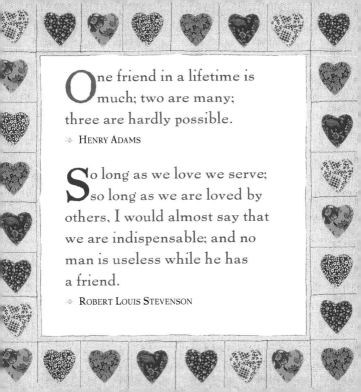

One friend in a lifetime is much; two are many; three are hardly possible.

HENRY ADAMS

So long as we love we serve; so long as we are loved by others, I would almost say that we are indispensable; and no man is useless while he has a friend.

ROBERT LOUIS STEVENSON

If a man does not make new acquaintances as he advances through life, he will soon find himself left alone. A man, sir, should keep his friendship in a constant repair.

◦ SAMUEL JOHNSON

A friend is the gift of God, and He only who made hearts can unite them.

◦ SOUTHEY

Wealth may crumble like some shaken tower, but friendship still remains. Disaster and defeat may overtake us and, like a shadow, hide our star, and our ambitions turn to ashes on our lips; but friendship, like some guardian angel, rekindles and fans into life the hope which had almost fled.

The comfort of having a friend
may be taken away, but not
that of having had one.

SENECA

I would not live without the love
of my friends.

JOHN KEATS

THE FRIENDLY THINGS

Oh, it's just the little homely things,
  The unobtrusive, friendly things,
The "Won't-you-let-me-help-you" things
That make our pathway light.

The "Laugh-with-me-it's-funny" things
And it's the jolly, joking things,
The "Never-mind-the-trouble" things
That makes the world seem bright.

For all the countless famous things
The wondrous record-breaking things,

These "never-can-be-equaled" things
That all the papers cite.

Are not the little human things,
The "everyday encountered" things,
The "just-because-I-like-you" things,
That make us happy quite.

So here's to all the little things,
The "done-and-then-forgotten" things,
Those "oh-it's-simply-nothing" things
That make life worth the fight.

AUTHOR UNKNOWN

Friendship is love without wings.

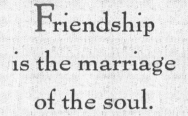

Friendship
is the marriage
of the soul.

So shall a friendship fill each heart
With perfume sweet as roses are,
That even though we be apart,
We'll scent the fragrance from afar.

GEORGIA McCOY

There is no folly equal to that of
throwing away friendship, in a
world where friendship is so rare.

BULWER-LYTON

To him that is afflicted, pity should
be showed from his friend.

JOB 6:14

It is my joy in life to find
At every turning of the road
The strong arms of a comrade kind
To help me onward with my load;
And since I have no gold to give,
And love alone must make amends,
My only prayer is, while I live—
God make me worthy of my friends.

❧ FRANK DEMPSTER SHERMAN

Two friends, two bodies with
one soul inspired.

❧ ALEXANDER POPE

The most I can do for my friend is simply to be his friend. I have no wealth to bestow upon him. If he knows that I am happy in loving him he will want no other reward. Is not friendship divine in this?

✢ LAVATIN

A friend loveth at all times, and a brother is born for adversity.

⊷ PROVERBS 17:17

There are no rules of friendship; it must be left to itself; we cannot force it any more than love.

⊷ HAZLITT

Friends are lost by calling often and calling seldom.

⊷ GAELIC PROVERB

Thus,
    God's bright sunshine overhead,
God's flowers beside your feet,
The path of life that you must tread
Can little hold of fear or dread:
And by such pleasant pathways led,
May all your life be sweet.

HELEN WAITHMAN

Do not judge, or you too
will be judged.

MATTHEW 7:1

Other blessings may be taken
away, but if we have acquired
a good friend by goodness, we
have a blessing which improves in
value when others fail. It is even
heightened by sufferings.

W. E. CHANNING

All who would win joy,
must share it; happiness
was born a twin.

LORD BYRON

We can never replace a friend. When a man is fortunate enough to have several, he finds they are all different; no one has a double in friendship.

SCHILLER

Of all happiness, the most charming is that of a firm and gentle friendship. It sweetens all our cares, dispels our sorrows, and counsels us in all extremities. Nay, if there were no other comfort in it than the bare exercise of so generous a virtue, even for that single reason a man would not be without it.

SENECA

When good friends walk beside us,
On the trails that we must keep,
Our burdens seem less heavy,
And the hills are not so steep,
The weary miles pass swiftly,
Taken in a joyous stride,
And all the world seems brighter,
When friends walk by our side.

❧ AUTHOR UNKNOWN

A friend is, as it were, a second self.

❧ CICERO

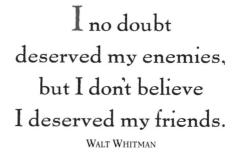

I no doubt
deserved my enemies,
but I don't believe
I deserved my friends.

WALT WHITMAN

Traveling in the company of those we love is home in motion.

LEIGH HUNT

H
old a true friend with both
your hands.

NIGERIAN PROVERB

P
erfume and incense bring joy to
the heart, and the pleasantness
of one's friend springs from his
earnest counsel.

PROVERBS 27:9

T
he best rule of friendship is to
keep your heart a little softer
than your head.

GEORGE SANTAYANA

The years. . .
    Have taught some sweet,
Some bitter lessons,
    None wiser than this,—
To spend all things else,
    But of old friends
To be most miserly.

JAMES RUSSELL LOWELL

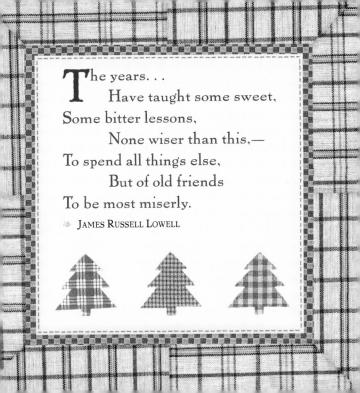

Friendship

improves happiness,
and abates misery,
by doubling our joy,
and dividing our grief.

JOSEPH ADDISON

Give me a few friends who will love me for what I am, or am not, and keep ever burning before my wondering steps the kindly light of hope. And though age and infirmity overtake me, and I come not in sight of the castle of my dreams; teach me still to be thankful for life and time's old memories that are good and sweet. And may the evening twilight find me gentle still.

AUTHOR UNKNOWN

Friendship is always a sweet responsibility, never an opportunity.

KAHLIL GIBRAN

Peace to you. The friends here send their greeting. Greet the friends there by name.

3 JOHN 14

Friendship consists in forgetting what one gives and remembering what one receives.

ALEXANDER DUMAS THE YOUNGER